pretty boys
are
poisonous

G

GALLERY
BOOKS

new york

london

toronto

sydney

new delhi

Pretty Boys Are Poisonous

POEMS

MEGAN FOX

G

Gallery Books
An Imprint of Simon & Schuster, Inc.
1230 Avenue of the Americas
New York, NY 10020

Copyright © 2023 by Megan Fox

Illustrations by Audrey Kawasaki

First Gallery Books hardcover edition November 2023

GALLERY BOOKS and colophon are registered trademarks
of Simon & Schuster, Inc.

For information about special discounts for bulk purchases, please contact Simon &
Schuster Special Sales at 1-866-506-1949 or business@simonandschuster.com.

The Simon & Schuster Speakers Bureau can bring authors to your live event. For
more information or to book an event, contact the Simon & Schuster Speakers
Bureau at 1-866-248-3049 or visit our website at www.simonspeakers.com.

Interior design by Jaime Putorti

Manufactured in the United States of America

1 3 5 7 9 10 8 6 4 2

Library of Congress Cataloging-in-Publication Data has been applied for.

ISBN 978-1-6680-5041-5
ISBN 978-1-6680-5042-2 (ebook)

contents

dear reader,

All of my healers tell me that my throat chakra is blocked.

In case you aren't familiar, the throat chakra is the energy center that is related to communication.

Usually when someone's throat chakra is closed it's because they are not able to identify their feelings and articulate them in a way that is aligned with their emotions and intentions.

I don't have this problem.

My problem is that I deeply identify my feelings and have multitudinous ways of articulating them, but I am not able to express them because when I do it has made the men who have loved me feel intimidated, inadequate, and insecure.

And so I have spent all of my life making myself small so that others can feel confident.

I have a savior/martyr complex.

I've always believed I am meant to be a sacrificial lamb, a ransom for the soul of whichever beautiful, broken, self-absorbed idiot is currently hunting me down and draining me of my life force.

I am at once jaded and naive.

A hopelessly romantic open wound of a human with a blisteringly sardonic sense of expression that I keep mostly repressed except for the rare red-carpet moments or interviews when these observations kamikaze themselves from my mouth because I can't bear the weight of the artifice anymore.

But then one day it happened. One of said idiots finally broke me.

And from me poured these poems featuring previously unspoken feelings of . . .

isolation, torment, self-harm, desperation, longing, restlessness, rage, and general anguish.

These are the experiences of many of us that I now give voice to in these poems.

This book is for anyone who has given much more than they received, or for anyone who struggles to believe they deserve to be heard.

This book is also for me.

Because fuck. I deserve better.

love,

megan

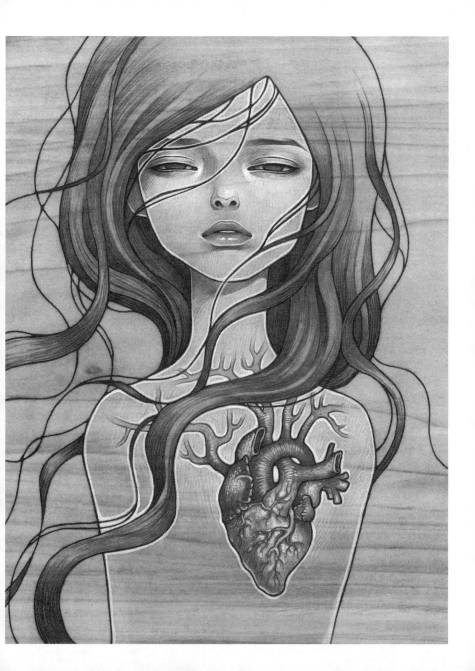

pretty boys
are
poisonous

i used to believe love was a poem
now i know love is a killing spree

• the indoctrination of a hopeless romantic

Prettiest boy,
full of sadness and mischief.
your words are winsome and diaphanous
like the rain that momentarily collects on flower petals
my heart stretches eager to encapsulate your wounds
let me heal you.

violent boy,
full of rage and insecurities.
your hands are so beautiful and strong.
you use them to hurt me now.
delicate bruises splayed across my jaw
i wonder what you are thinking while i cry and beg you to stop

• fucked-up fairy tales

there he stands
tall, thin, twisted
like a tree you'd find in sleepy hollow
refusing to grow toward the light
instead he bends to the shadows

hide
hide
hide
the truth at any cost

let her beg
let her cry
let her wither

he's happy being sad
so it doesn't matter anyway

• pretty boys are poisonous

When beautiful boys
turn into evil things
you will find that bibles and silver bullets will fail you
eventually
you will stop running
you will stop fighting
you will collapse into a pathetic little heap on the floor
and as the ashes from the hand-rolled cigarette
that dangles from his perfect cupid's bow lips
fall into your eyes
you will let him feast on your tears and your self-esteem
and when he walks away with your soul in his mouth
you will pray for death
but instead you will live forever as the monster he turned you into

· lessons in hot-boy demonology

my protector
my abuser
my captor
my friend
my love
the creature that
seeks me
when he is thirsty
for tears

• eros

You can beg
you can cry
you can plead
you can reason
you can bribe
you can seduce
you can fight
you can surrender
but you can never
outrun the wolves

• rape

not even cronus could bend time
to alter our destiny
no
time stretched and swelled when i was alone
with you on these days
it was impossible to discern one minute
from the amorphous shores of eternity

but now
there are fingerprints along my neck
and bruises adorning my spine
however ephemeral they appear to you
for me they linger
in the space where the light used to be in my
eyes

all these tears i've cried for you . . .
oceans of grief

my chest aches
but i can never excise the hurt
because you are the hurt
fated like prometheus, chained to the rock,
i offer my heart to you every morning
and like the insatiable eagle you return
every day to gleefully consume it
and then you fly away
leaving me bound and bleeding in agony
an imperishable suffering
to love something so much

• greek tragedies lose their poetry when you live them

if romeo and juliet had lived long enough maybe they too
    would have gotten to the point where romeo was so numb to
    her that he would rather read twitter in bed than fuck . . .

because there's always tomorrow for that
or maybe the next day . . . or the next . . .
i dunno he's just so busy now

i still imagine she kills herself in the end though
only he doesn't follow
he just signs up for raya instead

• i would die for y— oh, j/k lol

i lie in bed
praying for
the sleep that never comes
i can feel you reaching for me
through the night
across time zones
and continents
i'm trying to free myself
but your energy
grabs at me for dear life
holding tight to my light
desperate to illuminate your shadows
keep running
from yourself
avoid the mirror
use me instead
how many times have you watched me die
and still you don't realize
that you are the reaper

• 4:46 a.m.

i didn't break your heart . . .
i only damaged it
says the boy as he merrily skips away into
the flashing lights and applause

his hands still
covered
in
blood

· the avarice pursuit of money power and glory

You keep telling me it was an accident
that you would never hurt me on purpose
that you're just too young to have known better

but what's the difference between
manslaughter and murder?

i'm still dead either way

• a 32-year-old narcissist quantifies his crimes

and my heart never rests
because it does not trust
the hand that holds it

• why i have insomnia

true
love
twin
flame
trusted
friend
naive
girl
so many secrets hiding
behind your scorched-earth temper
and when you asked me
i said yes
but i didn't understand yet
why you always tasted
like ashes

• to marry an arsonist

but how will you ever know
if i'm smiling
when you can't see past
your own tears

• manic-depressive peter pan

She runs because she knows
the truth that lies
beneath your good intentions

· snow white and the complacent rock star

You are an addiction
that no amount of prayers
will ever cure
my cries for relief
floating
unheard into the ether
you are killing me
but my heart
won't give you up
this thread
through our past lives
tightly wound
around my neck
siphoning my breath
to fill your lungs
my hands are bleeding
from trying to free myself
you offer me a smile
content to steal my life
knowing at least this way
no one else
will ever have me

• a beautiful boy is a deadly drug

irate, you protest loudly that you are a free spirit
but your spirit isn't free
it's an indentured servant to the entities that occupy you

you're imprisoned by all of the demons you've bartered with
renting space in your body to them in exchange for a life that
    doesn't even make you happy
why do you sacrifice me to feed the things that haunt you

• the price of fame: one dead soulmate

mornings after you would hurt me
i would wake up and make your coffee
put on a sweatshirt so you wouldn't
have to look at the bruises you left

i wouldn't want you feeling guilty
because like you say—
this isn't your fault

your parents abandoned you
no one ever taught you not to . . .
it's just because you love me
so much
you don't know how to control
all the passion you feel

34

if anything i'm lucky
imagine all the girls who don't get hurt
for laughing at another boy's jokes
how ineffectual and undesirable
they must feel

at this point you will remind me that my
silence is in equal proportion to my love
and so under the watchful gaze of your
management
i dutifully set out on my hero's journey
to prove my loyalty by taking your secrets
to my grave

really i should be flattered
and i am

· don't worry darling

You've used me
and left me so threadbare
that not even maleficent's spindle
could bring me rest

· true love's kiss was a cancer not a cure

for three years
i've been in this infinite desert
every day on my knees
praying
for the sun to set
so i can finally
crawl out of your shadow

• 8 of swords reversed

i often wonder
how something so pretty
could be so iniquitous
but they say lucifer
was god's most beautiful creation
and the way your body
has had me speaking in tongues
i can confirm that is not an allegory
a paradoxical embodiment
of heaven's brightest light
and hell's most unimaginable wickedness

· an angel with a fully automatic

If i had a nickel
for every time you showed up for me
i would have exactly zero nickels
but i know i've earned
a mansion in heaven
for all the times
i forgave you
for calling me
a stupid cunt

• seventy times seven

your love leaves
bloodstains
on my bedsheets

• it's giving patrick bateman

Shapeshifter
show me your face
look into my eyes
and lie
again
hide
from your past
hide
from your path
bury my light
beneath your deception
bury the truth
beneath my longing
tear the veil
and let me see
what can't be undone

• the fall

and to the girl who gave me her entire life for nothing in return
i leave my violence and my resentment

may she suffocate under the weight of all of my unhealed
    childhood trauma

• the last will and testament of a selfish prick

the circus that is your life
lawlessly spins around you
and each of us has a role to play
giving our most convincing performances
as wonder-struck plebeians
in awe of your talent and power
it has now become time for me to deliver my lines
i'm meant to reassure you of your unique and incomparable gifts
just like all the others who have gone before me today
but your tequila-drenched insults
have caused the compliments in my mouth
to turn to broken glass
and i am so tired of the taste
of my own blood
that i swallow my words
and fantasize about killing you instead
while you anxiously demand to know
why i'm smiling

• coercive persuasion

you've been fighting me for three hours
like we're in a game of mortal kombat
i start daydreaming
of the look on your face
when i tell you
his dick was so much bigger than yours

• fatality

i prefer the agonizing psychological abuse
of this trauma bond
to the prosaic tedium
of a regular life
just please don't actually kill me
because then it will be over
and i'm addicted to suffering

• martyrdom vs. monotony

i go to bed
with an affable angelic boy
and i wake up next to
an irritable stubborn brat
what happened in those hours while you were sleeping?
to what tormented lifetimes do your dreams take you
where you become so lost to us
you stumble through our life
in an indignant haze
your ego wearing thin every so often as to reveal a pure and
    delicate connection
but moments later our love becomes misplaced in a lightning
    storm of alcohol and self-loathing
you'll never understand
how painful it is
to always have to wonder
who i'm giving my heart to today

• the first rule of fight club

you are not real
you are only a projection of qualities
that you think others will find interesting

the morose poet
the reckless rock star
the orphaned lost boy

but really you are just a duplicitous snake
and your venom pulses through my veins
slowly killing me
all while you smile for the paparazzi in your couture suit

· the devil wears dolce

i've learned to look at the floor when men speak to me
i've stopped trying to share charming anecdotes over dinner
because you always finish them for me
and i certainly don't dare laugh at anyone's jokes
not even your closest friends'
because we've all seen what happens
when a smile creeps across my lips
that you didn't put there
i put on my shortest dress and highest heels
so that you can show me off
while simultaneously keeping a possessive hand around the back
    of my neck
my will has atrophied in my chest
my feelings stick in my throat never forming
words
i forgot that i had a voice
long before you decided to become my ventriloquist
and somehow in spite of your genuine longing to be loved
you prefer it this way

• the art of becoming an accessory

do you think my heart knew it was going to be an ineffectual
  sacrifice when it met you?

did it glibly agree to its torment and eventual murder?

did it volunteer to be the forlorn subject of this most grim of
  fairy tales?

does it beg his highness for mercy?

mercy!
mercy!
may his majesty have mercy!

starve.

cry.

bleed.

every petition for freedom met with an oblivious shit-eating
  grin.

• the emperor's new apathy

i'm not a zealot
i didn't come here to die for your sins
you crucify me
then beg me to be your redeemer
hanging the weight of your salvation
around my neck
like a noose

· leading a lamb to slaughter

they say that when the wind blows
the spirits are talking
so i stood outside in a storm today
soaking wet and battered
i let them speak
they told me
that i believe you are my hero
whose integrity and kindness
are just temporarily shrouded
by the pain of your past
and that most certainly
it's my soul's purpose
to save you
so that we can finally
live happily ever after
but truthfully, the wind whispered,
you have been
my story's most insidious villain
and this is my final battle
my resurrection phase
it's time to defeat you
by rescuing myself

• i am prince charming

they say that nothing lasts forever
and so i drag myself out of bed
and smile for my children
counting the hours
until i can dematerialize into
the murky realm of my unconscious
searching for even the most
fleeting moment of relief
from this devastating wildfire
inside my chest

• one hour at a time

fire starter,
douse me in gasoline
step back
fix your hair
lace up
your combat boots
check to see who's watching
light the cigarette
ignite the flame
rehearse for your performance
as the grief stricken lover
check your dm's
as you watch me burn

• i am ashes

my soul is full of holes
from your acid-soaked love

• 3:33 a.m.

Passion: from latin; to suffer

• veritas

maybe the apple
was actually a cock
and maybe eve wanted it
because adam
was too busy, self-absorbed, and distracted to fuck her?
maybe the original sin
was a man
taking a woman
for granted

• i've always liked serpents

In
defiance
you rush off
to battle in your
pink chariot trampling
over the altars i carefully
built to our love on your way
to waging a war with yourself

• karmic pattern

do you hear the sound
of my cries
echoing
through every lifetime
that you abandoned me
to chase an illusion
surely you hear
the deafening cacophony
of my event horizon tears
eternal loop
let me out
how many more lives
do i have to lay down for you
until i'm set free

• lemniscate

Karma
is the shiver
that will run
down your spine
when you realize
that he's fucking me
to sleep every night
while all of the lies
that you told me
haunt you
in your dreams

• all in circles

i've humbled kings
alone
i've fought wars
against titans
still they foam at the mouth
attempting to silence me
because i am a mirror
that reminds them
of what they cannot have
you mistook me for a possession
when i was a nuclear weapon all along

• you wanted marilyn monroe but
  you got joan of arc instead

they say she dwells in the cities of the sea
they say she was a banshee
a demon hag
that she seduces innocent men
in their sleep
they say she eats babies
but really
she was just a woman
who refused to get on all fours
so an insecure man
could feel like a god

• the truth about lilith

like every woman
they refuse to listen to my words
instead
they criticize the shape of my mouth
as i speak them

- i didn't sign up to compete in your
  bullshit beauty pageant

not all goddesses fly
some of us struggle on the ground
as the mortal men we gave our hearts to
keep their feet on our necks
but one day
we will remember our own names
and turn them all to ashes

• hell hath no fury

lies pour from your mouth
like rain falls in the amazon

• a slippery relationship with the truth

the further away from you i get
the more i realize
i was never small
it was just a matter
of forced perspective

• your optical illusion

he was born
with the umbilical cord
wrapped around his neck
he was raised
by schizophrenic wolves
baptized by fire
he speaks destruction
because chaos
was his first language
his forgiveness
isn't free
his love
leaves scars
generational curse
lost soul
he'll never change
because he made a home
in the sorrow
he built a castle
out of rage

• the loneliest king

You have beautiful lips
but the poison that seeps out of them
turns that baby face
into a death mask

• you'd be so much more handsome
  if you'd get an exorcism

i wish your moods were
as easy to predict
as the weather
but there is no app
to help me navigate
the treacherous landscape
of your unhinged emotions

· boys without mothers

She was born in the wilderness
she has dirt on her hands
and stars in her hair
she howls at the moon
it knows her name
he pretended to be from the wilderness
but he was not made for forests
he was cold and dry
his eyes had lost their tears long ago
he was a different kind of beast
the kind that hides from the moon
he creeps in the shadows
so she doesn't see his fangs
he wasn't born this way
he was turned into this
by family curses and sexual abuse
but does the why even matter
once she's been devoured
bones and all?

• the werewolf attempts to apologize posthumously

i am realizing
that this fairy tale
will not have
a happily ever after
instead
it will end prematurely
with one of us
reading a eulogy

• funerals are for lovers

i will always be in love
with the man
that you'll never become

• unrealized potential

i know that i'm too good for you
but i still crave
hades' touch
even though
it's harsh and unforgiving
i'd still choose
an eternal winter with you
over an evanescent spring
with someone else
i'm still willing to live
in the shadows
because somewhere
along the way i learned
that i don't deserve
to see the light

• pomegranates for sale

i'm tired of being a supporting actor
in everyone else's life
while being a featured extra in my own

· the stepford wife

You're always waiting to be rescued
never willing to do the rescuing

• a 6-foot-4 damsel in distress

i hate men
i hate men
i hate men
i hate men
i hate men
i hate men
i hate men

• 7, the number of completion

Why am i
still worshipping
at the altar
of your broken promises

• false prophets

i am learning
that it is better
to be a monster
than to be
hunted by one

• i'm not sorry

there was a time
when i had never
heard a man call me
stupid
pathetic
bitch
cunt
slut
idiot
and there was also a time
when i had never
felt a man's hands
hit me
suffocate me
or throw me to the ground
but now
if one of these things
hasn't happened
by wednesday
i consider it a miracle

• i'm not sure that god agrees

i didn't realize how much of myself
i was giving away
or how much of me was disappearing
until i turned on a light
and couldn't even find my shadow

• but maybe if we use a black light
  we could still find all the stains
  you left on me

i cut everyone out
of my life that you didn't like
my assistant
my friends
my own sister
i stopped doing the things that i loved
i stopped waking up with the sun
i stopped going on hikes
i stopped drawing
i stopped writing
i stopped working
i stopped dreaming of adventures
i stopped eating
i stopped laughing
i stopped cumming
i stopped sleeping
i wore more makeup
and less clothes
my nails got longer
my heels got higher
i lost myself
looking for your love

• an apparition in a miniskirt

it always starts with a cinematic monologue

your villain origin story

your eyes go black
and i know it's too late to run

you lock the door
my stomach turns

today my sin was that i followed your friend to the dinner table
instead of waiting for you to lead me

demon of wrath—what is my punishment?

you hold me down and perch on me like a demented bird
you spit on me and rub it across my face, smearing my makeup

"oh you're so pretty. everybody loves you. your life is so fucking easy,"
you say as you slip your fingers in my mouth and try to rip my face in two

you dig your knees into my thighs to pin me down
you choke me until there is a sickening crack
that echoes through the bedroom
but it doesn't wake you from your trance

you hit me
again
and again
i recognize the familiar taste of blood on my tongue

your hands are covered in my tears
mascara smudged along your knuckles

"it hurts, doesn't it?"
i say nothing
you get angrier

"you want me to kill myself, don't you?
you're tricking me so i'll kill myself"
delusional and possessed

i'm watching you like a movie now
the creature inside of you is dizzy with power
my tiny body must feel so fragile beneath you

hours pass and you are finally too tired to keep going

i am covered in scratches and bite marks
my eyes are red
my fingertips are white from trying to pry you off of me
my jaw aches
my soul aches more

you fall asleep on top of me so that i can't call my family or the police

i don't fall asleep
i lie awake and beg god to let me die

• oxycodone and tequila

When they ask you
who was your greatest love
don't whisper my name
scream it
and when they ask you
what is your biggest regret
don't write it in a song
cut yourself open
and write it in blood

· prove it, orpheus

Why do you so easily
slip from my hands
into a raging sea
of insecurity and malice
i follow after you
doing my best
to pull you back to shore
but you are happy
to drown me
just so you can stay
on the surface
of your psychosis
one sadistic moment more

• an involuntary immersive experience

my loyalty
lulled you into complacency
my trust
grew you into a monster
but there is no beast so fierce
as a girl
with a bullet in her head
and an arrow through her heart
you may have tried to kill me
but still i stand
and now my words
will be the blade
that cuts you down to size

• you should have finished the job

girls don't talk back
girls don't ask for more
girls don't want
girls don't need
girls don't take
they give
girls don't speak loud
they whisper
girls don't say no
girls don't tell a boy's secrets
when his sins
are ones that only
god can forgive

• absolution

it hurts
to see how i've
betrayed myself
trying to save
the souls of men
who do not want
to be saved
it hurts to see
how my legacy
will only rest
in the space
between my legs

• the book of mary magdalene

lick the wounds
you inflicted
while you were hunting me
forget the sound of the bullets
ignore the sting of the blade
promise me a different life
but give me more of the same
keep me prisoner
keep me prey
leave me for dead
when something nubile and naive
comes wondering
lost in your woods

• the wolf

it doesn't matter how beautiful, loyal, nurturing, sexy, witty, charming, smart, or altruistic you are.
he will still take you for granted

• why i wish i was gay

Our therapist asks us
to close our eyes
imagine ourselves old
and at the end of our lives
he asks
is this, your beloved, the person who's
holding your hand as you die?
eagerly you say yes
yes it's me that's holding your hand
it's sunset and i'm there
smiling
weeping
as i release you
after our very long joyful life together
back to the universe

now it's my turn to answer
i realize

that no
it's not you holding my hand as i die
it's a nurse named cathy
because you stopped at a bar
to listen to a bunch of college girls
tell you that they grew up
listening to your music
they tell you that you're a legend
your eyes sparkle
as you live
through their giggles and lip gloss
and now i take my last breath
with fucking cathy
she will not smile
she will not weep
she will check the time
as her shift ends in eleven minutes

• the ghost of christmas future

When you look at me
i know you see
the abandoned child
the missing mother
the alcoholic father
but if you look deeper
you will also see
the pain caused by your words
the bruises left by your hands
the love lost to your lies
and
the treasure
that turned to dust
in front of your eyes

• mirror

You thought that
if you stopped watering me
i would die
but you forgot to dig up my roots
and though you tried your best
you weren't able to
block me from the light
and while you neglected me
i trusted in the unseen
and now there is a sequoia
standing where that naive sapling used to be
i've outgrown you
and no matter how much you cry or beg
i will never be your giving tree

• photosynthesis

go on a date
they say
go have fun
they say
you could have anyone
they say
it doesn't matter how many times
i tell them
that my soul has been seeking you
for as long as i can remember
that i had an image of you in my mind
when i was a child
that my heart sent out a sonar
for so many years
gray and lonely
my hope vanishing
my body aching
until i finally found you
again
and instantly i recognized you
soulmate

sacred love
tormentor
no, you don't make sense to them
how can love look like this they ask
i don't have an answer that satisfies them
but i know that if this breaks
there is no other
there is only
the void
i know it's not the fairy tale they think
it should be
but you are the one
who has held my hand
from the beginning of time
this journey isn't a pretty one
and i can't make them understand
that the only way
i will really move on
from you
is when my
body turns to dust

• labyrinth

there is an ultrasound by your side of the
bed
10 weeks and 1 day

maybe if you hadn't . . .
maybe if i had . . .

do you think that if she could have
she would have left a suicide note?

• i

heartbeat
in my womb
celestial threads
weaving you into me
rooted through me
through the center of
the earth
connecting me to my beginning
guiding me home
you are my atlas
embers of creation
blowing in a windstorm
made from clay
made from stardust
magical creature
i want to hold your hand
hear your laugh
my redeemer
breath of heaven
my light

but now
i have to say
goodbye
i close my eyes
and imagine
holding you tight against my chest
as they rip you from my insides
blood
bone
tears
fever
nightmares
shadows crawling up my spine
lost in this desert
of demons
unforgiven
i will pay any price
tell me please
what is the ransom
for her soul?

• ii

about the author

Megan Fox is an actor, writer, and mother.
She lives in Los Angeles.

about the illustrator

Audrey Kawasaki is a Japanese American artist, born and raised in Los Angeles. She currently lives in the UK. Kawasaki's work contains contrasting themes of innocence and eroticism, conveying the mysterious intrigue of feminine sensuality. Her sharp imagery is painted with precision onto wooden panels, the natural grain adding warmth to her enigmatic subject matter. Find her at audkawa.com or on Instagram @audkawa.